SPAWN

SPAWN

MARIE-ANDRÉE GILL

Translated by Kristen Renee Miller

Book*hug Press
Toronto 2020
Literature in Translation Series

FIRST ENGLISH EDITION

Published originally under the title
Frayer © 2017 by La Peuplade, Chicoutimi, Canada
English translation copyright © 2020 by Kristen Renee Miller

Printed in Canada

The production of this book was made possible through the generous assistance
of the Canada Council for the Arts and the Ontario Arts Council. Book*hug
Press also acknowledges the support of the Government of Canada through
the Canada Book Fund and the Government of Ontario through the
Ontario Book Publishing Tax Credit and the Ontario Book Fund.

Book*hug Press acknowledges that the land on which we operate is the
traditional territory of many nations, including the Mississaugas of the Credit,
the Anishnabeg, the Chippewa, the Haudenosaunee and the Wendat peoples.
We recognize the enduring presence of many diverse First Nations, Inuit and
Métis peoples and are grateful for the opportunity to meet and
work on this territory.

Library and Archives Canada Cataloguing in Publication

Title: Spawn / Marie-Andrée Gill ; translated by Kristen Renee Miller.
Other titles: Frayer. English
Names: Gill, Marie-Andrée, author. | Miller, Kristen Renee, 1982– translator.
Series: Literature in translation series. | Description: First English edition.
Series statement: Literature in translation series | Poems. | Translation of: Frayer.
Identifiers: Canadiana (print) 20200158856 | Canadiana (ebook) 20200158880
ISBN 9781771665971 (softcover) | ISBN 9781771665988 (HTML)
ISBN 9781771665995 (PDF) | ISBN 9781771666008 (Kindle)
Classification: LCC PS8613.I439 F7313 2020 | DDC C841/.6—dc23

our dead do not take flight
except within ourselves
like children we bear
who clear a path to the interior

Paul-Marie Lapointe
Tr. Kristen Renee Miller

We the unlikely
the aftermath
the remains of heart muscle
and black earth

We the territory
in a word

We have learned to avert our gaze, grow
beautiful as airplane graveyards

to grin at winning bingo cards

Spawn
straight from the scar
spawn

THE RAMPART

At the lake, the fish we're looking
for is the ouananiche. In Ilnu:
she who is found everywhere
or little lost one.

if I don't touch the sidewalk lines
if I keep on running
till I reach the third street light
everything will be fine

it isn't real it's in my head it's nothing
my strong nails
will cling to this disorder

the lake eats away a little more cement with bleeding

                                                        gums

and I want this whole thing over with
like that first french on the rampart

(we are everywhere lost)

some benches
some pruned cedars
and there, looming
four cement teepees

engraved:
beaver
snowshoes
canoe, bear
drab cement
drab procession
the story drawn, lifeless

The rampart

suspended in time
prams, drunk boys

day and night the dogs

day and night the dandelions push
through cracks in the cement

and before us, the lake
a luck
the lake.

its flashing waves
revive humanity
one drop at a time

on the main street
we draw game migrations
and curves of the stock exchange in chalk

we cherish the thrill of plucking daisies
and count the petals silently
to be sure that someday
we'll be loved

We have plans for you, they say.
And we laugh. As narcotic ghosts cling
to the storms of our bodies
we laugh.

THE RESERVE

In early summer, the ouananiche returns
to her native river, a tributary of the lake,
where she lives large in the cold,
clear waters at rock bottom.

I am a village that didn't have a choice.

to lick the skin of the water
with a tongue I don't speak

the day lifts me up on his shoulders to watch
the varnish half-stripped from our memories
the cement pelt poured over our feral skins

how to augur anything
but crooked miracles
anyway

A luck: the arena at night and making out
behind the police station
the northern lights dancing on nintendo
chicken buckets, the monthly allowance
happy meals from nobody's birthday
and weekends in the woods
and partridges to twist.

And the lake, a luck, the lake.

only one thing takes the edge off: fresh water

the main beach
Boivin Bay, the dip
the community site
the rampart steps
past the stone spikes
l'Île aux Couleuvres
the outboard motorboat
the fibreglass canoe
astride a blue styrofoam
or a pitoune

(all the nicer beaches charge a fee)

To smooth the rift, words

that moment nobody tells me
what I should look like.

In houses all alike women embroider your future
on moccasins sold to tourists.
The light comes and goes.

Timushum says: *Only thunderstorms still tell it
like it is.*

I got up early to watch the sun
fuck with the lake
I pinched an eyelash in my fingers, drank your face
straight from the bottle
the possibilities have become too much
for me

what to do with your hide: ply it
tan it
by hand, by cartridge clip

up close, our animal skin
looks like any other

How do you swallow the lake's beauty with all these ghosts chewing through its plastic-filled lung. I'm in the underwater level of a video game just as the air runs out, just as that little tune begins to play.

inhaling a one-night to clear my head
the rivers, tattooed from within, unclean
as snorting stars
from the bathroom sink

I need the lake to take me

(get me out of these fifteen square kilometres)

endlessly seek
what to make of your skin

through skid roads and byways
and cemetery shortcuts
seek

seek

This impression of laughing too hard:
our power.

I want the America that cries out in your voice
I want our plundered bloods
our earth-coloured, powwow bloods
rising in her throat
when she sees us queuing
for the microwave.

Balsam fir dance in slow motion and the earth
shudders as I come
as my fingers find the burning ember.

I want this vertigo as a vow
to sap the cruel beauty
of oil-slick rainbows.

ADOLESCENCE

Almost always, the ouananiche
survives the spawning.

behold the prize at the bottom of twenty-four:
no longer able to count up to mauve
and the fear of possibility and *all the things*
I'll never do
if I can't find
the other north

I'm nothing when I wake up without panties
and my monthly answers me like a knife

can't remember last night
it's class photo day

me too can't wait for you to leave your foster family even
if last time I said I didn't when you grabbed my ass I love
you all the same we just have to stop talking about it and
it'll be okay *love u 4-ever* it's written in my diary it's written
on the benches the cement the trees

the little heart closes like a dandelion in darkness
seagulls tread water in the wind
of your badlands of your brush fires of your hands
around my neck

Playing with a thumbtack in math class.
Sucking blood from a name
etched in my arm.

to fend off death, the ten of us suck
a cock-shaped bong
since we exist only to laugh at ourselves
and seek ourselves in the night

come I'll take you to my room to make love
for the first time
which I will not remember

I'll sneak out my window Friday
and we'll find someone to get us beer

we'll hit an arcade
and I'll lose my head over you
but we'll have a story, us two
even if we lack the words
to tell it

we are the world
but we don't know it

splashing our good clothes
stringing you along

you'd be—
I'd be—
and then we'd go—
and then we'd do—
and then— I'd tell you
and then— I'd say

we learn by heart
the logic of nodes
of inordinate knowledge

the internet probes the twilight
in our ruby-throated eyes
no longer capable of flight

People have incredible colours

their hides painted
by the sun.

sometimes the sky pulls down his starry leggings
and comes hot
in the lake's wide mouth

it's always there, that colour
of mixed diesel pulsing
through the two-stroke organs
of our winter bunkers

a luck
your joie de vivre
orangeade in a squirt gun
to smooth the rifts that time
has already scraped down my hide

our smoke-scented dreams sketch
a flock of snow geese
on the ceiling of possibility

I have a ski-doo on asphalt at night
in my belly
with all its shooting sparks

light pulses through the prism
of our colliding bodies
rose, rose-coloured as always

(no one takes a brush cutter
to the remains of lost loves)

he left with
just his cock and his knife
to be reincarnated multicoloured
into a muskrat promise

And when the night draws its celebrations to a close, the hares undress all alone, sexes smeared from long storms. Perhaps we've forgotten that the body, yes the body, finds a desolate kind of beauty once exposed.

PIEKUAKAMI: THE LAKE

Adult ouananiche have a choice:
return to the lake or winter
in the great troughs of the river
to descend again in spring.

I seize the ice by its haunches
the lake, tangled in its own light
cracks its knuckles in every crevasse

we bathe in the malaise
of hot asphalt
waiting for a habitable word
waiting to win the scratch-off lottery
and take to the woods forever

digging a finger through the rampart's fresh cement
writing a name, never the same one
before the lake and its gills of raw sky
where the wind whistles a country song forever

it's time to sober up
from the thirst for certain waters

who knows the colour of a sore throat
cut loose

a lynx drags her claws
down the tender gullet walls
of the ones who drown
before birth

now voilà
we have these yellow-orange floats
and seal fins
to open up our eyes

splitting the surface of the lake
stripping the pelt from its shoulders
where sweetwater salmon drink
the milk of our fallow hearts

we cut our teeth on weapons
I know we are blue plumage
the symmetry of spruce
the language of hailstones

eating cold corned beef at inhuman hours
choking on long macaroni at night
I leave a name behind at the border
at the edge of my disorder

with a trace of the love bite on my neck

drinking rain from clay
all the vodka of the fjord

rubbing balloons in our hair
we will spread a little more ketchup
on the human wound
and birth a spring-
time of seven-up gone flat

ouananiche revive the watercolours
of our blooming organs
time to swallow the evidence
of our mutant hides

the ten-centimetres-dilated code of etiquette:
it's to quit pretending
it's licking the plate and the bones
until nothing is left but the echo
of our laughter or raptors waiting to devour
the future

it's burden enough to be born
between sheer vertebrae of ice
to not live by strict timetables

here we cherish chaos
as humanity's bright future
happy to get this bleak life
for just a few easy payments

we come
from savage beasts
and the same light
learning by heart pell-mell
the inhibition of pain

we have hundreds of years
of cataclysm at hand
there are signs installed side by side
in the chalky veins of the nomadic life

the accumulation of our gaze:
centuries

(I'm just trying to resemble
this ancient water of which I am the child)

Meeting the blue-grey gaze
of the nearly bursting lake

we see our dream: a woman risen up
from all these winter worlds
heaped with ice, ready to start again.

Ouananiche remain in the lake, while Atlantic salmon migrate to the sea for part of their life cycle. With the exception of this difference, ouananiche and Atlantic salmon are the same species.

TRANSLATOR'S NOTE

to lick the skin of the water / with a tongue I don't speak…

Marie-Andrée Gill's *Spawn* is a surprising, colourful, virtuosic collection. Its brief, untitled poems span '90s-kid nostalgia, the life cycle of freshwater salmon, a coming of age, and the natural landscape of the Mashteuiatsh reserve, centred on Lake Piekuakami—a site of recreation and commerce, a reminder of conquest and ecological decline, a symbol of the ancient world, of sex, of the cycles of life. These poems are tightly interdependent, and *Spawn* could truly be read as a single, braided, book-length poem. But I want to focus here on a theme that became especially vital to my project of understanding and translating the book: recovery of language.

In Gill's Mashteuiatsh community in Quebec, the native language of Ilnu-aimun is spoken as a first language by only about seventeen per cent of residents, French by eighty per cent. It's no surprise, then, that *Spawn*, published originally in French, is a text acutely aware of its existence and discomfort within a settler language. In *Spawn*, the young Indigenous speaker longs for a *parole habitable*[1]. She "lick[s] the skin of the water / with a tongue [she doesn't] speak." She knows a story but not "the words to tell it." She inscribes the world around her, carving words into wet concrete, into tree trunks, into her own skin.

As *Spawn*'s translator, tasked with rendering the text from one settler language (French) into another (English), my work was delicate and intense. The poems in *Spawn* work to subvert the language in which they're written, to resist its conventions. Gill starts poems in the middle of sentences, in the middle of thoughts. She capitalizes and punctuates according to an internal logic, then breaks her own rules. She interrupts her own finely tuned sonic play with dissonance and elevated diction with slang. She resists containment; she resists categorization; she resists her French-speaking readers. She unsettles.

In English, I have worked to preserve the tension of Gill's choices: her reversals of convention, her shifts in register, her project of disruption. I've worked to render in English a voice as sensitive and intimate as it is raw and elemental. For Gill's speaker, the recovery of this voice, this identity, this *parole*, is a life work. As she asserts in one of the book's final poems, "We cut our teeth on weapons / I know we are … the language of hailstones."

---

1. A home-like, habitable, livable language; a bearable speech; a survivable word.

ACKNOWLEDGEMENTS

From the author:

Tshinishkumitin Jonathan Lamy and Max-Antoine Guérin for the help and poetic vision.

Tshinishkumitin Mylène Bouchard, Simon Philippe Turcot, and Sophie Gagnon-Bergeron of La Peuplade. You are hot.

Tshinishkumitin Kristen Miller for translating my work, and Jay and Hazel Millar of Book*hug Press for publishing it in English.

Thank you to the Canada Council for the Arts.

From the translator:

All my thanks to my publishers, Jay and Hazel at Book*hug Press, and to the editors at *The Kenyon Review*, *The Common*, *Guernica*, *The Offing*, and *Tupelo Quarterly*, who published selections from *Spawn*.

And my thanks to the organizations whose support helped make this project possible: the Kenyon Review Writers Workshop, the Kentucky Arts Council, the Kentucky Foundation for Women, Fund for the Arts, Vermont Studio Center, and Blackacre Conservancy.

PHOTO: SOPHIE GAGNON-BERGERON

Marie-Andrée Gill is Pekuakamishkueu and identifies primarily as a poet. Mother, friend, lover, student, her research and creative work concern transpersonal and decolonial love. Bridging kitsch and existentialism, her writing is rooted in territory and interiority, combining her Quebec and Ilnu identities. She is the author of three books from La Peuplade: *Béante*, *Frayer*, and *Chauffer le dehors*. In 2018 she was the winner of an Indigenous Voices Award. She lives in L'Anse-Saint-Jean, Quebec.

PHOTO: AMBER ESTES THIENEMAN

Kristen Renee Miller's poems and translations appear in *POETRY*, *The Kenyon Review*, *Guernica*, *The Offing*, and *Best New Poets 2018*. A recipient of fellowships from The Kentucky Arts Council, Vermont Studio Center, Blackacre Conservancy, and the Kentucky Foundation for Women, she lives in Louisville, Kentucky, where she is the Managing Editor at Sarabande Books.

COLOPHON

Manufactured as the first English edition of
Spawn
in the spring of 2020 by Book*hug Press

Copy edited by Stuart Ross
Cover by Tree Abraham
Text by Jay Millar

bookhugpress.ca